Toward
Socialist America

Toward
Socialist America

An Analysis of America's Slide into Collectivism

Communism, Fascism, and Nazism are all major variants of the underlying ideology called Collectivism. *Collectivism* vs. *Individualism*

Robert D. Gorgoglione Sr.

To order additional copies of this book, contact:
Xlibris Corporation
1-888-795-4274
www.Xlibris.com
Orders@Xlibris.com
84846

CONTENTS

APPENDIX

The American people will never knowingly adopt Socialism; but under the name of liberalism, **they will adopt every fragment of the Socialist program** *until America will one day be a socialist nation without knowing how it happened.*

Norman Thomas, six-time Socialist Party candidate for President

*Americans may not be willing to vote for a program under the name of "Socialism," but put it under another party label—***whether liberal Republican or Democrat***—and they're by and large in favor of the idea . . . .*

Earl Browder, General Secretary of the Communist Party USA

1995—Revised & expanded, March 17ᵗʰ, 2010. Call 1-208-357-4294

"The State is all!"

"Every man's life is at the call of the nation and so must be every man's property. ***We are living today in a highly organized state of socialism. The state is all;*** *the individual is of importance only as he contributes to the welfare of the state. His property is his only as the State does not need it.* ***He must hold his life and possessions at the call of the State.***"

Bernard Baruch
Advisor to Franklin Delano Roosevelt's New Deal.

"Everything for the State, nothing outside the State, ***Nothing above the State!***"

Benito Mussolini
Fascist dictator of Italy

"We are socialist, *we are enemies of today's capitalistic economic system . . . , and we are all determined to destroy this system unde4r all conditions."*

Adolph Hitler
National Socialist dictator of Germany

"Every new local or federal public ownership project is an added nail in the coffin that will finally contain capitalism."

Joseph Stalin
Communist dictator

"That" Explained Stalin *"is Communism"*.

"*Joseph Stalin advised the late William Z. Foster* that the American people would never accept socialism or communism and that *the only hope of imposing a Red regime in the United States was 'a consistent but gradual increase in local and federal public ownership projects'*. Publicly-owned operations, he pointed out, paid little if any taxes and in the end ' . . . *result in a final acceptance of complete government ownership and operation.' That, Stalin explained, is communism.*

"*'Every new local or federal public ownership project,' said Stalin, 'is an added nail in the coffin that will finally contain capitalism.* The tax burden will become greater every year for the American people, and each government-owned operation will throw an added burden on the private taxpayers. *It is obvious that the camel's back of capitalism will finally break under an unbearable burden.'* Stalin told Foster ' . . . *that the average left-wing American liberal,* who would be insulted at being called a Socialist or a Communist, would enthusiastically use all of his influence to bring about more and more public ownership operations in the field of natural resources, transportation and other commercial lines. **That is the way *we must enlist the left-wing liberals* in all walks of life**, not only in the United States, but in all Latin America as well."

Howard E. Kershner
Christian Economics, 4/17/62

"We are *enemies* of today's capitalistic economic system . . ."

"*We are socialist, we are enemies of today's capitalistic economic system for the exploitation of the economically weak, with its unfair salaries, with its unseemly evaluation of a human being according to wealth and property instead of responsibility and performance, and we are all determined to destroy this system under all conditions.*"

Adolph Hitler

A Prophetic Warning from the Past

The Prophet **Joseph Smith . . .** spoke of the rise of subversive organizations in the last days, and warned against them. In speaking of such developments, *John Taylor said in 1881*:

> *"I am sorry to see the murderous influence prevailing throughout the world, and perhaps this may be a fitting occasion to refer to some of these matters. The manifestations of turbulence and uneasiness which prevail among the nations of the earth are truly lamentable . . . . These feelings which tend to do away with all right, rule, and government, and correct principles are not from God, or many of them are not. **This feeling of communism [socialism] and nihilism, aimed at the overthrow of rulers and men in position and authority, arises from a spirit of diabolism, which is contrary to every principle of the Gospel of the Son of "God.***
>
> *"These things are beginning to spread among and permeate the nations of the earth. Do we expect them? Yes. **These secret combinations were spoken of by Joseph Smith, years and years ago**. I have heard him time and time again tell about them, and he stated that when these things began to take place, **the liberties of this nation would begin to be bartered away.** We see signs of weakness which we lament, and we would to God that our rulers would be men of righteousness, and that those who aspire to position would be guided by honorable feeling—to maintain inviolate the Constitution and operate in the interest, happiness, well-being, and protection of the whole community. But we see signs of weakness and vacillation. **We see a policy being introduced to listen to the clamor of mobs and of unprincipled men** who know not of what they speak, nor whereof they affirm, **and when men begin to tear away with impunity one plank after another from our Constitution, by and by we shall find that we are struggling with the wreck and ruin of the system which the forefathers of this nation sought to establish in the interests of humanity."*

John Taylor
Journal of Discourses, Vol. 22, Pages 142-143

"DOCTRINAL COMMENTARY ON THE PEARL OF GREAT PRICE"
By Hyrum L. Andrus, Deseret book Company, Salt Lake City, 1972
Chapter 12; page 420

WHAT IS SOCIALISM
(Collectivism)?

Economic control of people by government.
See—Part 1: The Chasm

Since there are several major variants of Socialism, it is important to begin with a good definition:

> **Socialism:** *Government* **control and/or ownership** *over the basic means of production and distribution of goods and services.*

> Or simply: ***Economic control*** *of people by government.*

In order for government to regulate and control economic activity, **it must first control people,** for it is people buying and selling in the market place that make up the economy.

The above definition of Socialism includes *democratic socialism*, *Fascism* [Corporate Socialism], *Nazism* (National Socialism) and *Communism* (International Revolutionary Socialism).

It was over 40 years ago that I began to realize that the United States had already moved far down the soul-destroying road of Socialism. Little did I realize that I was not alone in coming to such an unpopular and *"politically incorrect"* conclusion.

Let's turn to the evidence that will prove that **we are and have been on the road toward a Socialist America since at least 1933 (Roosevelt's New Deal).**

Bernard Baruch, Wall Street financier and key advisor in Franklin Delano Roosevelt's New Deal and chairman of the War Industries Board during the First World War, stated the following in an August 1918 speech:

Every man's life is at the call of the nation and so must be every man's property. **We are living today in a highly organized state of socialism. The state is all;** *the individual is of importance* **only** *as he contributes to the welfare of the state. His property is his only as the State does not need it.* **He must hold his life and possessions at the call of the State**. (**The New American** *magazine," **The One Party State"**, Oct. 4, 2004) **The one-party state:** *the Republican National Convention . . .*

Baruch would have made a great speech writer for Hitler, Mussolini and Stalin!

Baruch's statement is not at all as extreme as it sounds when one takes into account the amount of socialistic regimentation and controls congress and President Woodrow Wilson's administration put on American industry and resources during World War 1. (**War Collectivism and World War I** by Murry N. Rothbard)
War Collectivism in World War I

In 1936, in an attempt to show the striking parallels between the Socialist and Democrat Party platforms, Al Smith, a former democratic presidential candidate, declared:

Make a test for yourself. Just get the platform of the Democratic Party and . . . the Socialist Party and lay them down . . . side by side and . . . **scratch out the word Democrat and scratch out the word Socialist and let the two platforms lay there.**

ROBERT D. GORGOGLIONE SR.

EARL BROWDER

"America is getting socialism on the installment plan"

Earl Browder, then general secretary of the Communist Party USA, in an address before the National Press Club in Washington D.C., in August of 1936, told assembled reporters:

> *The program of the Socialist Party and the program of the Communist Party have a common origin in the document known as the Communist Manifesto. There is no difference, so far as the program is concerned and final aim . . .*
> **See *The Communist Manifesto***

The Socialists follow the lead of the Communists, the Democrats follow the lead of the Socialists, and the **Republicans follow the lead of the Democrats.** At the end of the road is complete Socialism which is Communism. *Before we can go Communist, we must first go socialist.*

In 1966, 30 years later, Earl Browder was quoted in the *Pittsburgh Press* as follows:

> **America is getting socialism on the installment plan through the programs of the welfare state.** *There is more real socialism in the United States today than there is in the Soviet Union [Union of Soviet **Socialist** Republics].*
>
> *Americans may not be willing to vote for a program under the name of "socialism," but put it under another party label—**whether liberal Republican or Democrat**—and they're by and large in favor of the idea . . .*
>
> *We have no real socialist party, no socialist ideology, but we have a large-and growing-degree of what 50 years ago would have been recognized as socialism.*

NORMAN THOMAS

"The United States is making greater strides toward socialism . . . "

"In 1928 Thomas made the first of his six consecutive races for the presidency. However, the Socialist party continued losing strength, ending the decade as a minor element in America's political system. As the Socialist candidate for president every 4 years, **Thomas at least had the *satisfaction* of seeing much of his program *taken over by Franklin Roosevelt's New Deal*."** *Norman Thomas: Biography from Answers.com*

By 1953 Norman Thomas was Jubilant. He wrote a pamphlet called, *Democratic Socialism* **in which he stated that:**

> " . . . *here in America more measures once praised or denounced as socialist have been adopted than once I should have thought possible short of a socialist victory at the polls."*

By the mid 1950's**, Norman Thomas,** six time candidate for President of the U.S. on the Socialist Party ticket, proclaimed that **practically all of the planks of the Socialist Party platform of 1932 had been adopted by both the Democrat and Republican parties**.

In 1957, the *"Harvard Times-Republican"* **of April 18** quoted Norman Thomas as follows:

> *"The United States is making greater strides toward Socialism under Eisenhower than even under Roosevelt, particularly in the fields of Federal spending and welfare legislation."*

In 1962 Norman Thomas summed up the whole situation as follows:

"The difference between Democrats and Republicans is: Democrats have accepted some ideas of Socialism cheerfully, while Republicans have accepted them reluctantly." (***Cleveland Plain Dealer***, October 19, 1962.)
(From page 130 of *The Naked Capitalist*, A review on Dr. Carroll Quigly's Book: *Tragedy and Hope*, Published privately by Dr. Cleon Skousen, 1970)

On July 14, 1969, *U.S. News and World Report* noted:

*"The late Norman Thomas, who ran unsuccessfully for President six times on the Socialist Party ticket, observed in 1964 that the Democrats "have through the years taken over measures once regarded as Socialist, but then so have the Republicans but to a slightly less degree." The **Republican** Platform of 2000*

HAS THE U.S. ADOPTED THE "TEN POINT PLANK" OF THE COMMUNIST MANIFESTO?

In order to comprehend, more fully, just how far down the Socialist road (under both Democrat and Republican presidents) we have traveled, consider the following extracted from the **Ten Point plank of the Communist (Socialist) Manifesto of 1848:**

1. *Abolition of property in land and application of all rent of land to public purposes.* (Confiscation and ownership of vast areas of land by both the Federal and state governments with the remaining private lands under multiple restrictions and regulations.)

2. *A heavy progressive or graduated income tax.* (The Federal Income Tax was adopted in 1913. Many of the states have since adopted their own versions of the graduated income tax.)

5. *Centralization of credit in the hands of the state, by means of a national bank with state capital and an exclusive monopoly.* (The Federal Reserve Banking System is a national bank with a very powerful and "exclusive monopoly.")

6. *Centralization of the means of communication and transport in the hands of the state.* (i.e. government FCC regulations on radio and television and the ICC regulations on the railroads, trucking companies, and the airlines etc. Amtrak is owned by the Federal Government. Some bus and transportation services are owned by state governments and regional metropolitan areas.)

10. *Free education for all children in public schools.* (Government schools, colleges and universities. *A Layman's Look at the* **Communist Manifesto**
The Ten Planks of **the Communist Manifesto** *Translated*

WERE WILLIAM Z. FOSTER'S PROPOSALS ["TOWARD SOVIET AMERICA"] ADOPTED IN THE UNITED STATES?

In 1932, William Z. Foster, Chairman of the Communist Party USA authored the book ***Toward Soviet America.*** Beginning on Page 277 he declared that there would be:

> . . . . *revolutionary* **nationalization** *or* **socialization** [such as environmentally restrictive controls and regulation] *of the large privately-owned . . . factories, mines and power plant, . . . railroads, waterways, airways, bus lines* [and] . . . *the whole body of forest, mineral deposits, lakes, etc.* (National Parks and forests etc.)

On page 281, he added:

> *There will also be . . . social insurance against unemployment, old age* [Social Security] . . . . *free medical services* [Medicare, Medicaid & Socialized Universal Health Care.] . . . *All houses and other buildings will be socialized.* [government zoning, planning and safety regulations etc.]

Now comes the shocker beginning on pages 316—317:

> *Superstition* [religion] *will vanish in the realm of science; . . . class ideologies . . . will give place to scientific materialist philosophy* [Humanism]. . . . . *the schools, colleges and universities will be grouped under the National* [Federal] *Department of Education . . .* **studies will be revolutionized being cleansed of religious, patriotic, and other features of bourgeois** [middle class] *ideology.*

> *Science will become materialistic, hence truly scientific:* **God will be banished** *from the laboratories as well as* **from the schools.** . . . . *there will be a great organization of science, backed by the full power of the government.* [Sound familiar?]

On page 318 we read:

A National Department of Health [the Department of Health and Human Services] *will be set up. A free medical service . . . will be established.* (Socialized Universal Health Care).

Foster—**Toward Soviet America**—*The* **Book** *the Communists Tried to . . .*

Speak Up For Truth: **Toward Soviet America**

The **Communist Takeover** *of America: 45 Declared* **Goals** *. . .*

HAS THE UNITED STATES ADOPTED PORTIONS OF THE "NATIONAL SOCIALIST WORKERS PARTY" PLATFORM?

Now we come to the National Socialist (Nazi) parallels that exist in the United States. Many of the famous *Twenty-five Points* of the National Socialist German Workers Party (NAZI) has been **echoed by both Republicans and Democrats alike. Here are a few:**

1. . . . . *provide work* and the means of livelihood for the citizens of the state . . . .

2. *We demand an extensive development of provision for old age.* (Social Security).

3. *The State must undertake a thorough reconstruction of our national system of education, with the aim of giving to every capable and industrious [citizen] the benefits of a higher education . . . . We demand educational facilities for specially gifted children of poor parents . . . at the expense of the State.* (Think of the Federal "Goals 2000" and "No child left behind." etc.)

4. *The State must concern itself with raising the standard of health in the nation . . . .* (Socialized Universal Health Care, Medicare, Medicaid, etc.)

5. *The Party . . . is convinced that our nation can only achieve permanent well-being from within on the principle of placing the common interest before self-interest.* (Special interests and "group rights" replace "individual rights.")
National Socialism, Platform Planks of

Other points included such things as—are you ready—**gun control [registration and confiscation]**, federal welfare, and yes, day-care. They even had their own National Endowment for the Arts.

Stephen H. Roberts wrote:

The Fuhrer was fast establishing "der totale Staat"; there was forced unionization . . . price-fixing, myriad Welfare programs, and a federal takeover of education. Credit expansion and "public works" programs helped to create the myth of full employment. Hitler organized that current "Liberal" panacea, a national health service, in which care was "centralized, and the Department was given surprisingly wide powers. It looked after the health of children and workers; it controlled the training of doctors and midwives and dentists and chemists; . . . (**The House that Hitler Built,** New York, Harper & Brothers, 1938)

Now we will let Adolph Hitler have the last word:

We are socialist, we are enemies of today's capitalistic economic system for the exploitation of the economically weak, with its unfair salaries, with its unseemly evaluation of a human being according to wealth and property instead of responsibility and performance, and we are all determined to destroy this system under all conditions. **(Speech of May 1, 1927. Quoted by J. Toland in** *Adolph Hitler,* **Garden City, N. Y.: Doubleday.)**

Why Nazism Was Socialism and Why Socialism Is Totalitarian
The Origins of Nazism—Ludwig von Mises—Mises Institute

STRIKING SIMILARITIES BETWEEN FDR'S "NEW DEAL" AND MUSSOLINI'S FASCISM (CORPORATE SOCIALISM)

James Henry writing in *The New Australian* on January 24th, 1999, noted that:

> " . . . the vast majority of people are totally incapable of recognizing a fascist economic program, even when it is used to slap them in the face. This is because they have not been taught that **fascism means state direction of the economy**, cradle to grave 'social security', **complete control** of education, **government intervention** in every nook and cranny of the economy — and the belief that **the individual belongs to the state**. *American Fascism Liberal Fascism Explained*

Webster's Unabridged Dictionary defines **Fascism as:**

> *Any program for setting up and centralizing an autocratic regime with severely authoritarian politics **exercising regulation of industry, commerce and finance**, rigid censorship, and forcible oppression of opposition.*

Charlotte Twight's scholarly *America's Emerging Fascist Economy* (Arlington House, 1975 page 20), points to Fascist Pretenses about property rights, which are in turn abrogated by license, regulation, limiting competition etc. Twight explains that:

> *To sustain its power and achieve its economic ends, fascism seeks to make its people **economically** and **psychologically dependent** on the government. [This] enhances the governments . . . control over its' citizen's economic activities.*

> *Fascism also installs the **mandatory government license as a central economic weapon,** for **compulsory government licensing** of businesses allows the political hierarchy to control the nation's economy **without the appearance of totalitarian coercion.**

*Altruistically phrased, vague **licensing standards** such as the national or community interest, local needs, or the personal qualifications of the applicant **preserve a facade** of justice and due process **to conceal unlimited governmental power.** Exactly such elastic standards for **government licenses prevailed** in Nazi Germany. **Charlotte Twight**: The Independent Institute*

Unfortunately, these same Corporate Socialist controls and regulations are now in full bloom here in our beloved country, the United States of America.

Many of the principles of Mussolini's Italian **Fascism** as well as Hitler's German **National Socialism** have also been adopted in the United States **by both the Republican and Democrat Parties.** Please notice that what follows has ***striking parallels*** to what we have already covered!

It was Franklin Roosevelt, a Democrat, who wrote:

I have wanted the . . . government, above all, to give great care to the social legislation needed to carry out our part of agreed international programs for industry and for those who bear the future of industry . . . in fact, it has ratified the laws for the eight-hour day, for obligatory insurance, for regulation of the work of women and children, for assistance and benefits, for after-work diversion and adult education, and finally for obligatory insurance against tuberculosis. All this shows how, in every detail in the field of labor, I stand by the . . . working classes. All that it was possible to do without working an injury to the principle of solidarity in our economy I have set out to do, from the minimum wage to the continuity of employment, from insurance against accidents to indemnity against illness, from old age pensions to the proper regulation of military service. There is little which social welfare research has not already been advanced by me. I want to give every man and woman so generous an opportunity that work will be not a painful necessity but a joy of life . . .

Pure "New Deal" philosophy!

Now I have to confess. The author of the foregoing was not Roosevelt. It was the Socialist Benito Mussolini. (***My Autobiograhy***, **New York,**

Charles Scribner's Sons, 1928). You have to admit that it sure sounds like Roosevelt.

In *Architects of Conspiracy* **by William P. Hoar,** on page 127, we find the following shocker:

> *The economics of Fascist Italy were soon being imported into this country by President Franklin D. Roosevelt, whose C.C.C., W.P.A., P.WA. and other Depression-era schemes proved so damaging. Indeed,* **in his 'memoirs' former President Herbert Hoover told it as it was:** *'Among the early Roosevelt fascist measures was the National Industry Recovery Act (NRA) of June 16, 1933 . . . .* **[these ideas]** *were adopted by the United States Chamber of Commerce.** During the campaign of 1932, Henry I. Harriman, president of that body, urged that I agree to support these proposals, informing me that Mr. Roosevelt had agreed to do so.* **I tried to show him that this stuff was pure fascism; that it was a remaking of Mussolini's corporate state** *and refused to agree to any of it. He informed me that in view of my attitude, the business world would support Roosevelt with money and influence. That for the most part proved true.* **(Western Islands, 1984)** *William P. Hoar—Architects of Conspiracy (Table of Contents)*
> *Amazon.com:* **Architects of Conspiracy***: An Intriguing History . . .*

As was the case in corporate socialist Italy, and NAZI Germany, American corporations were financing and organizing corporate socialism right here in the United States in an effort to consolidate and control, i.e., monopolize, the wealth and productivity of the American economy for themselves. This was the essence of the "New Deal"
The People's Pottage
The Revolution Was—Garet **Garrett***—Mises Institute*

It should also be made clear that Nazism and Fascism are classified as **Corporate Socialism**, a political and economic system **by which giant corporations and banks maintain their monopolistic control of a nations economy** through government regulatory regimentation, *licensing* and financial control. That is, government intervention—ism, which encourages *monopoly capitalism*, thus limiting or even destroying the competition of *competitive free enterprise capitalism*. Remember, **socialism is not a** share-the-wealth program, but is in reality, a tool by which monopoly capitalists consolidate and control the wealth for themselves.

F. A. Voigt, a foreign correspondent prior to and during World War II, wrote:

> . . . *Marxism* [Socialism] *which has led to Fascism and National Socialism, because, in all essentials, it is Fascism and National Socialism.*

Nobel laureate **Friedrich A. Hayek** stated: *"Basically National Socialism and Marxism **are the same**."*

Omnipotent Government, by Ludwig von Mises (Table of Contents)
***Socialism** by Ludwig von Mises FRIEDRICH AUGUST VON HAYEK*
Now we will let Benito Mussolini have the last word:

> *"Everything for the State, nothing outside the state, nothing above the state.*

> *"**Fascism** should more appropriately be called **Corporatism** because it is **a merger of State and corporate power**."* (In other words, **Corporate Socialism!**)
> ***American Fascism Fascism** Revisited*

Now for the Republicans.

As we shall see, many Republicans also have been and are supporting these corporate socialist principles and programs.

RICHARD NIXON'S "GREAT SOCIALIST REVIVAL"

One of the most startling articles ever to appear in an American magazine appeared in the **September 21, 1970 issue of** *New York* **Magazine entitled** *"Richard Nixon and the Great Socialist Revival."* by the very liberal (socialist) **Harvard economics professor John Kenneth Galbraith.**

Galbraith began by proclaiming:

> *Certainly the least predicted development under the Nixon Administration was this* ***great new thrust to socialism***. *One encounters people who still aren't aware of it. Others must be rubbing their eyes, for certainly the portents seemed all to the contrary. As an opponent of socialism, Mr. Nixon seemed steadfast . . . .*

Further on in his article, Galbraith writes:

> *But I had come reluctantly to the conclusion that socialism, even in this modest design, was something I would never see. Now I am being rescued by this* ***new socialist upsurge*** *promoted, of all things, by socialists not on the left but on the right. And they have the blessing, and conceivably much more, of a Republican Administration.*

Professor Galbraith, in making reference to the British Fabian Socialist *"doctrine of the commanding heights"* **wrote:**

> *The new conservative socialism in the United States has taken over the strategy of the commanding heights with a vengeance.*
> (*Nixon: The Man Behind the Mask*, Western Islands, 1971)

Two additional testimonies of President Nixon's great thrust into Socialism are found in *"None Dare Call It Conspiracy"* **by Gary Allen:**

"Walter Trohan, columnist emeritus for the *Chicago Tribune* and one of America's outstanding political commentators, has accurately noted:

> *It is a known fact that the policies of the government today, whether Republican or democratic, **are closer to the 1932 platform of the Communist Party than they are to either of their own party platforms in that critical year.** More than 100 years ago, in 1848 to be exact, Karl Marx promulgated his program for the socialized state in the Communist Manifesto . . .*

"And Mr. Trohan has also been led to believe that the trend is inevitable:

> *Conservatives should be realistic enough to recognize that **this country is going deeper into socialism** and will see expansion of federal power, whether Republicans or democrats are in power. The only comfort they may have is that the pace will be slower under Richard M. Nixon than it might have been under Hubert H. Humphrey . . .*

> *Conservatives are going to have to recognize that **the Nixon Administration will embrace most of the socialism of the Democratic administrations,** while professing to improve it . . .*

"Fellow Harvard socialist Dr. Arthur Schlesinger has said much the same thing:

> *The chief liberal gains in the past generally remain on the statute books when the conservatives recover power . . . liberalism grows constantly more liberal, and by the same token, conservatism grows constantly less conservative . . .*

> (*None Dare Call It Conspiracy* by Gary Allen, Concord Press, 1971, (Chapter 2)
> *NONE DARE CALL IT CONSPIRACY* by *Gary Allen*
> mhp: **Socialism**: *Royal Road to Power for the Super-Rich*

It was during the Nixon Republican administration that the following steps (among others) toward Socialism were taken:

1. The socialistic **Environmental Protection Agency** was created by an unconstitutional executive order, thereby circumventing Congress, and giving the federal government virtual control and power over all land, air and water.

2. **Federal Revenue Sharing,** which has led to a greater and more direct federal control of state and local governments, and therefore greater socialistic concentration of political and economic power.

3. The total and complete **elimination of any remaining gold backing of our currency** which has further facilitated the weakening of the value of the dollar, thereby creating greater price inflation (rising prices).

4. Socialistic **price controls** leading to growing shortages which nearly led to rationing.

5. Greatly increased **treasonous foreign aid,** trade and financial credit and loans to our communist enemies. (Particularly Soviet Russia and Communist China.)

6. Greatly increased spending for unconstitutional socialistic programs such as social services, entitlements, medical care, education, foreign aid and other socialistic transfer-of-the-wealth schemes etc. (The sharing of someone else's wealth, of course—**legal plunder.**)

And lastly, Richard Nixon's economic and fiscal policies can be summed up as follows:

"I am now a Keynesian in economics"—**Richard Nixon**
The Trouble With Keynes | *The Freeman* | *Ideas On Liberty*

Was President Nixon a socialist?
*Republican Infiltration in Gary Allen's **Nixon*** | *Erik Fortman*

So now you can see clearly that both the Republican and Democrat Parties have become very effective vehicles for pushing the United Stated toward complete socialism. Unfortunately the process continued even under the George W. Bush administration.

"... a Republican administration will continue and complete the work of a Democratic (Clinton) administration."

One of the major policy areas where President Bush was continuing and expanding the work of the Clinton administration is in the area of socialistic environmental regulation. Bush stated:

*And now, a Republican administration **will continue and complete the work** of a democratic administration.*

Of course this statement can be applied to most if not all major policy objectives such as:

1. **Education:** In January 2002, President Bush signed into law the "No Child Left Behind Act," which radically increased the federal role in education. In his most recent budget proposal, the fiscal 2005 budget, Mr. Bush proposed spending $64.3 billion for the Department of Education, as compared to $35.7 billion in 2001, the year he assumed office — an 80.1 percent increase.

2. **Foreign Aid:** In March 2002, President Bush called for a 50 percent increase in "core development assistance" over three years. In his fiscal 2005 budget, he proposed $16.6 billion in total spending for "international assistance programs," as compared to $11.8 billion in 2001.

3. **Agriculture:** In May 2002, President Bush signed into law a gargantuan farm bill he supported that increases direct farm program spending by $73 billion over 10 years and also contains $243 billion for food stamps.

4. **Health Care:** In December 2003, President Bush signed into law a new prescription drug entitlement program he championed. When passed by Congress, the administration estimated that the program would cost $400 billion over 10 years. Subsequently, the administration revised the $400 billion estimate upward to $530 billion. (*The New American* **magazine,** *"Whom Do We Elect"*, **July, 12, 2004),** *Not Yours To Give by Walter Williams — Capitalism Magazine*

For a preview of what a second Bush administration would do to continue expanding on the **socialistic** policies and programs of the previous Clinton democratic administration, hear what *liberal* Republican columnist **Andrew Sullivan** had to say:

> *The (2004 GOP Convention) began with a series of speeches trumpeting vast increases in federal spending: on education, healthcare, AIDS, medical research, and on and on, . . .* **No, these were not Democrats. They were Bush Republicans,** *extolling the capacity of government to help people, to cure the sick, educate the young, save Africans from HIV, subsidize religious charities, prevent or cure breast cancer, and any other number of worthy causes.* (**The New American** **magazine,** **"The One Party State",** **October 4, 2004)** *The one-party state: the Republican National Convention . . .*

"George Bush Becomes a Socialist!"

> *"We live in a wonderfully ironic world.* **George W. Bush might have now nationalized more companies than Hugo Chavez.** *He certainly has nationalized companies with far greater worth. Fannie Mae, Freddie Mac and now AIG. Let alone the bailouts of Bear Stearns and all the rest.*

> **"Who knew George Bush would turn out to be such a socialist? You might even argue, communist.** *What happened?*

> *" . . . but I believe in capitalism. So, George Bush's socialism is wigging me out. He privatizes the army but socializes the mortgage industry. I understand how this came about, but does Bush have a plan? Do they have*

*any idea how they are going to get out of this **business or are they planning on running a quasi-socialist government from now on?***

*"**If other industries head south, will Bush nationalize those too?** Who has more nationalized companies now — the US or Russia?" (**George Bush Becomes a Socialist!** Cenk Uygur, **The Huntington Post,** September 17, 2008) Cenk Uygur: George Bush Becomes a Socialist*

"There ought to be limits to freedom."
Governor George W Bush, May 21, 1999

President Bush IS a Socialist! *March 8, 2004 | New American, The | Find Articles at BNET*

Notice how much these programs parallel those of NAZI Germany, Fascist Italy and **William Z. Foster's** *Toward Soviet America*.

Now we come to President Barack Hussein Obama and what appears to be the final drive into full blown communism and the final end of the United States, Constitutional government and American civilization.

"WE ARE ALL SOCIALIST NOW"

President Obama's Marxist-Communist background and associations; Completion of the Socialist-Communist Revolution.

With the mighty push by the Obama administration to simultaneously in-act Cap and Trade, socialized health care, hate crimes legislation and real ID etc, there seems to be a growing feeling among many that we are in the midst of a final drive into full blown communism and the final end of the United States, Constitutional government and American civilization.

Before we can discuss the above bold statement, it is very important to understand where Obama is coming from and to have a knowledge of his background and past and present associations.

Consider: Barack Obama *was born of* Marxists; mentored by a communist writer and activist; spent his college days hanging around radical and Marxist activists; worked as a radical community organizer, learning the radical tactics of the communist, Saul Alinsky; was introduced to Chicago politics by a communists and today lends his political skill to the international goals of communist activists, and had communist working on his campaign and now in his administration.

Obama has surrounded himself with racists, socialists, Marxists, communists Such as Van Jones, Anita Dunn and Ron Bloom etc and domestic terrorists and accused felons.

The fact is, Obama has been around Marxists (communists, of one kind or another), since the age of 12. *www.theobamafile.com DAMAGING DISCLOSURES IN VAN JONES SCANDAL*
*Another **Mao Lover in the White House**?*

On 11/25/2008, the Communist Party USA congratulated Barack Obama for his electoral victory on there web site as follows:
Congratulations on an extraordinary history making election!

We can think back with pride to decades of hard work toward our strategic goal of a big enough, broad enough and united enough labor and all-people's movement that could overcome the ultra-right blockage to all progress. That the people's movement has come to life, it is dynamic and it has the potential to keep growing. The election of Barack Obama and a strengthened Congress creates new conditions in our country. There is now the possibility to shift gears and move forward. This new day requires us to further develop our tactics in order to continue to deepen and broaden labor and people's unity.

There are thousands of experiences that we all have had in these momentous days, some large, some small, all of which express the enormity of change in thinking and readiness for involvement that is underway and that steels us for the battles ahead. **Communists: Obama 'best opportunity in decades'**
(See *www.worldnetdaily.com*)

The tears of joy we all shared as crowds gathered to watch the election results here and throughout the world dramatize the new moment we are in. **www. cpusa.org** *Cliff Kincaid —* **Communist Party Backs Obama**
(See Cliff Kincaid at ***www.newswithviews.com***)

When communists start crying "tears of joy," it certainly removes all doubt, doesn't it?

Now comes a real surprise from the mouth of Soviet Communism.

On May 19, *Pravda,* the Moscow Communist daily newspaper presented an editorial under the title of "***American capitalism gone with a whimper.***" It declared in part:

"It must be said, that like the breaking of a great dam, **the American decent into Marxism** *is happening with* **breath taking speed**, *against the back drop of a passive, hapless sheeple, excuse me dear reader, I meant people".*

"The final collapse has come with the election of Barack Obama. His speed in the past three months has been truly impressive. His spending and money printing has been a record setting, not just in America's short history but in the world. If this keeps up for more then another year, and there is no sign that it will not, America at best will resemble the Wiemar Republic [of 1920's Germany] and at worst Zimbabwe." American capitalism gone with a whimper—Pravda.Ru

Ironically, "Pravda" is the Russian equivalent of the English word for "truth"!

Consider the following news report from *Reuters* of June 2, 2009.

CARACAS (Reuters)—*Venezuela's **President Hugo Chavez** said on Tuesday that he and Cuban ally Fidel Castro risk being more conservative than U.S. President Barack Obama as Washington prepares to take control of General Motors Corp.*

***During one of Chavez's customary lectures** on the "curse" of capitalism and the bonanzas of socialism, the Venezuelan leader made reference to GM's bankruptcy filing, which is expected to give the U.S. government a 60 percent stake in the 100-year-old former symbol of American might.*

*"**Hey, Obama has just nationalized nothing more and nothing less than General Motors. Comrade Obama! Fidel, careful or we are going to end up to his right,**" Chavez joked on a live television broadcast.* [Seriously; this is NO JOKE !]

*During a decade in government, Chavez has nationalized most of Venezuela's key economic sectors, including multibillion dollar oil projects, often via joint ventures with the private sector **that give the state a 60 percent controlling stake**.*

Chavez has nationalized Venezuela's economy industry by industry. Is Obama trying to follow his lead? **Is this not exactly what Obama is doing at present?!** It seems that Obama has the affection of ruthless Communists. See **chavez** and **comrad** *obama*

Some major examples of Obama's thrust toward a Socialist-Communist state are as follows:

1. *Universal socialized national health care* which would destroy what is left of the private health care industry.

2. *"Cap and Trade"* which would drive up the cost of energy and destroy what little is left of our once mighty industrial base.

3. *Nationalization of the banks*.

4. *Massive "bailouts"* leading to Nationalization of American industry and finance

5. *"Stimulus packages"* leading to a massive expansion of the welfare state and greatly increased dependence [slavery] upon "The State" by the American people for sustenance and lively hood.

6. Establishment of a compulsory Marxist *"National-Community Service"*.

7. Setting up a Marxist *"National Civilian Security Force"* which would enable the Federal Government to dramatically increase its control over the population (**"Civilian Defense Force"**).

8. The final completion of the economic and political integration and merger of the United States into the *"New World Order"* by way of a unification with a *"North American Union"* or *The European Union*. This would be the end of the United States as an independent and sovereign nation.

The Communist's version of this "New World Order" was issued by the official *1936 program of the Communist International*, an arm of the Kremlin, is as follows:

Dictatorship can be established only by a victory of socialism in different countries or groups of countries [**European Union, North American Union etc.**] after which the proletariat [Communist] republics would unite on federal *lines with those already in existence* [Russia, China etc.] *and this system of federal unions would expand at length forming the "World Union of Socialist Soviet Republics."* (**Hearings before the Senate Committee on Foreign Relations, July 11, 1956 p. 196 and** *The Fearful Master: A Second Look at the United Nations* **by G. Edward Griffin, Western Island, 1964.)** *Council On Foreign Relations CouncilOnForeignRelations.net Stop the North American Union www.cfr.org*

The above program was further developed by *William Z Foster, National* **chairman of the Communist Party, U.S.A., from 1933-1957, when he wrote:**

A Communist world will be a unified, organized **world** [**world government-integrated socialized world economy**]. *The economic system will be one great organization, based upon the principle of planning now dawning in the USSR. The American soviet government will be an important section in this world government . . . .* (**William Z. Foster,** *Toward Soviet America,* **Balboa Island, California, Elgin Publications, 1961, pp. 326-327.)** *United States* **Foreign Policy**

I dare to submit to you, the reader, that all of the evidence presented thus far is proof that there is a Conspiracy to destroy our sovereignty, and independence as well as the glorious Constitution of our beloved country.

What has and is now unfolding before our very eyes is NOT the results of incompetence, ignorance or stupidity. It is CONSPIRACY! As John Birch Society founder Robert Welch once stated, it is "brilliant cunning". We see now that he has been vindicated!

Based on the above evidence, we must dare to ask the question that many would consider unthinkable, but then "*truth is some times stranger than fiction*"!

QUESTION: **Is Barack Hussein Obama a Communist?**

The Communist program is still in effect and nearing completion and the history of the last 56 years has vindicated Senator Joseph McCarthy! *Conservative* **Book** *Service:* **Blacklisted by History** *by M. Stanton Evans* (Crown Forum, Random House 2007).

CONCLUSION AND SOLUTION

In conclusion, a very good way to measure the growth and advance of socialism in these United States is to look at the growth of federal spending and the size of the Federal budget. It took well over 100 years for the federal budget to reach about **1 billion dollars in 1917**, just before entering the First World War. 45 years later in **1962, it reached about 100 billion.** Now, 48 years later, in the year 2010, under a Democratic administration, the federal budget is now over *4 Trillion dollars* **with 3 trillion dollar deficits and growing**. Even with price inflation factored in, this is astronomical. Lest we forget, the national debt is now approaching the **13 trillion dollar level!** Now if you think these figures are staggering, start adding up the exploding growth of all state and local spending and debt. **U.S unfunded liabilities (debt) is over 107 trillion.** *U.S. National Debt Clock : Updated in Real Time*
www.goldsilver.com www.thenewamerican.com
Grandfather Federal **Government Debt Report**—*page 2—by MWHodges*

Now imagine how prosperous and rich we would all be had the Federal Government's spending been frozen at the 100 billion dollar level of 1962, while being forced to return to its strict Constitutional limitations. **(See, *Article I, Section 8 of the U.S. Constitution and Amendment X of The Bill of Rights.*) *NOT IN THE CONSTITUTION***
***Thomas Jefferson on Politics & Government Elliot's Debates* of the Const. Conv.**

All of the above is a perfect description of the political and economic realities that exist in the United States today! In Nazi Germany, Fascist Italy, and the Union of Soviet **Socialist** Republics, socialistic and welfare-state ideas were developed in the name of socialism. But here in the United States, socialism was promoted in the name of: "social reform," "social justice," "equality," "civil rights," and liberalism, etc.

Republican and Democratic administrations come and go, **but the show remains the same.** The rapid growth and increasing size of tyrannical taxes, printing press money (inflation of the currency.) very burdensome regulatory controls and the loss of most of our precious God-ordained rights to individual liberty continue **no matter which party is in power.** The lock-step march toward **complete socialism (Communism)** continues unabated.

We Americans should never forget the wise counsel of the Father of our beloved country, **George Washington:**

> *Government is not reason; it is not eloquence;* ***it is force****; like fire, it is a* ***dangerous servant and a fearful master.***

It was for this very reason that **James Madison** wrote the following in **Federalist Paper No. 25:**

> *The* ***powers delegated*** *by the proposed Constitution to the federal government are* ***few and defined****. Those which are to remain in the State governments are* ***numerous and indefinite****. The former will be* ***exercised principally*** *on external objects, as war, peace, negotiation and foreign commerce. . . . The* ***powers reserved to the several States*** *will extend to all the objects which in the ordinary course of affairs, concern the lives and liberties, and properties of the people, and the internal order, improvement and prosperity of the State.*

And now this from the great **Thomas Jefferson:**

> *. . . . it would be a dangerous delusion were a confidence in the men of our choice to silence our fears for the safety of our rights; that confidence is everywhere the parent of despotism;* ***free government is founded in jealousy and not in confidence****; it is jealousy and not confidence which prescribes limited constitutions* ***to bind down those whom we are obliged to trust with power****; that our Constitution has accordingly fixed the limits to which* ***and no further*** *our confidence may go; . . . . In questions of power, then let no more be heard of confidence in man* [officers of government] ***but bind them down from mischief by the chains of the Constitution. The Kentucky Resolutions*** *of 1798*
> *Jefferson on Politics &* ***Government: Republican*** *Principles*

If we as a people and a nation do not return to those *principles and precepts of our divinely inspired Constitution* and Competitive Free Enterprise System, *and once again worship the God of the land, who is Jesus Christ,* we will pass into oblivion and history as have other great civilizations before us.
An Ageless Constitution Based On Lasting Principles The Federalist Papers Declaration of Independence, U.S. Constitution, Historical Do.

But let us not despair. There is still great hope if we will but seek wisdom and counsel from the great Benjamin Franklin who was instrumental in helping to guide and steady the Framing Constitutional Convention of 1787 to a great and successful conclusion. At a time when the Convention was on the verge of breaking up, and the new infant nation was close to sliding into anarchy, as is the case for us today, **Benjamin Franklin gave the following wise counsel:**

> *We indeed seem to **feel our own want of political wisdom**, since we have been **running about in search of it** . . . In this situation . . . **groping as it were in the dark to find political truth** . . . how has it happened, sir, that **we have not hitherto once thought of humbly applying to the Father of lights** [God] **to illuminate our understandings?** . . . I have lived, Sir, a long time, and the longer I live, the more convincing proofs I see of this truth—that God governs in the affairs of men. And if a sparrow cannot fall to the ground without his notice, **is it probable that an empire can rise** [or survive] **without his aid?** . . . Henceforth [let us pray for] **the assistance of Heaven, and its blessings upon our deliberations** . . .* (Constitutional Convention, 1787) *The Miracle at Philadelphia*

It was with the assistance and inspiration of Heaven that our Forefathers settled this choice land and brought about the birth and rise of this nation with faith and great sacrifice. Now may we follow their great example, and walk in their footsteps; pick up where they left off and restore our divinely inspired Constitution and thus our beloved country to its former greatness and glory; that **we may once again be a shining light of Liberty and hope for a world in spiritual darkness and physical bondage,** *for this is our destiny!*
Leading America to Victory | *New American, The* | *Find Articles at BNET*
www.thenewamerican.com   www.jbs.org   www.stopthenorthamericanunion.com

---

MY OATH OF ALLEGIANCE
TO THE CONSTITUTION

I do solemnly swear that I will support and defend the Constitution of the United States against all enemies, foreign and domestic; that I will bear true faith and allegiance to the same. Since God provided that in this land of liberty, my political allegiance shall run not to individuals, that is, to government officials, my allegiance and the only allegiance I owe as a citizen of the United States, runs to our inspired Constitution which God himself set up. A certain loyalty I do owe to the office which a man holds, but I owe no loyalty to the man himself. This principle of allegiance to the Constitution is basic to our liberty. Our Constitution is the Supreme Law of our Land; that any laws or statutes conflicting with it are "Null and Void" (See Art. 1, Sec. 8 and Amen 10 and Article VI.)

I now pledge to follow the great example of our Founding Fathers and walk in their footsteps; pick up where they left off and, if necessary, sacrifice all that I have to restore our divinely inspired Constitution, and thus my beloved country and Republic to their former greatness and glory; that we may once again be a shining light of Liberty and hope for a world in spiritual darkness and physical bondage—FOR THIS IS OUR DESTINY!

Robert D. Gorgoglione Sr.

THE FOUNDERS INCLUDED LIMITATIONS ON TAXES AND SPENDING IN THE CONSTITUTION

April 15, 2009 Great Idaho Falls Tea
Party flyer by Robert D. Gorgoglione

Our Senators and Representatives take an oath to *"defend the Constitution of the United States against all enemies, foreign and domestic"*, and to *"bear true faith and allegiance to the same,"* but do they really mean it?

Consider the following:

> *"Each report of a committee on a bill or joint resolution of a public character shall include a statement citing the **specific powers granted** to the Congress in the Constitution to enact the law proposed by the bill or joint resolution."*
> (From the Rules of the House of Representatives.)

But how do we determine what the *"specific powers granted"* are? It's very simple; the specific powers granted to Congress are listed in **Section 8 of Article I, Clauses 2 through 17.**

Clause 1 of Section 8, better known as "The Welfare Clause", contains the following:

> *"The Congress shall have power to la4y and collect taxes, duties, imposts and excise: to pay the debts and provide for the common defense and general welfare of the United States . . . "*

Nowhere in Clauses 2-17 of Sec 8 will you find any grants of power to appropriate monies for "the general welfare" in the form of boondoggles such as bailouts, Foreign aid, entitlements, welfare, farm subsidies, state grants, aid to education, housing, student grants, Social Security, Medicare and Medicaid, etc. The list is endless.

If there is anything else the Framers of the Constitution forgot, Amendment 10 says you can't do that either. The Great Thomas Jefferson quotes and qualifies the Tenth Amendment as follows:

> *"I consider the* **foundation of the Constitution** *as laid on this ground: That* **'all powers not delegated to the United States, by the Constitution, nor prohibited by it to the States, are reserved to the States, or to the people.'** *To take a single step beyond the boundaries thus specially drawn around the powers of Congress,* **is to take possession of a boundless field of power, no longer susceptible of any definition."**

In other words, **"*a boundless field of spending and taxes*", along with controls and regulations, which stifle initiative and productivity. *Think of a budget of 100 billion, rather than 3.5 trillion!!!!***

APPENDIX

MONOPOLY CAPITALIST

The following excerpts from the late *Antony Sutton*, former Research Fellow at the Hoover Institution for War, Revolution and Peace at Stanford University from 1968 to 1973, will give *greater insight* and *historical perspective* to the above work.

" . . . it may be observed that both the extreme right and the extreme left of the *conventional* political spectrum are absolutely collectivist. The **national socialist** (for example, the fascist) and the **international socialist** (for example, the Communist) *both recommend totalitarian politico-economic systems based on naked, unfettered political power and individual coercion.* **Both systems require monopoly control of society.** While monopoly control of industries was once the objective of J. P. Morgan and J. D. Rockefeller, by the late nineteenth century the inner sanctums of Wall Street understood that **the most efficient way to gain an unchallenged monopoly was to "go political"** and *make society go to work for the monopolists* — **under the name of the public good and the public interest.** This strategy was detailed in 1906 by Frederick C. Howe in his *Confessions of a Monopolist.*[1] Howe, by the way, is also a figure in the story of the Bolshevik Revolution."

"Consequently, one barrier to mature understanding of recent history is the notion that all capitalists are the bitter and unswerving enemies of all Marxists and socialists. This erroneous idea originated with Karl Marx and was undoubtedly useful to his purposes. **In fact, the idea is nonsense. *There has been a continuing, albeit concealed, alliance between international political capitalists and international revolutionary socialists — to their mutual benefit.*** (See *The Rockefeller File* by Gary Allen, Chapter 9—Building The Big Red Machine, Concord Press, 1976)

This alliance has gone unobserved largely because historians — with a few notable exceptions — have an unconscious Marxian bias and are thus locked into the impossibility of any such alliance existing. The open-minded reader should bear two clues in mind: *monopoly capitalists are the bitter enemies of laissez-faire entrepreneurs;* and, **given the weaknesses of socialist central planning,** *the totalitarian socialist state is a perfect captive market for monopoly capitalists,* if an alliance can be made with the socialist power brokers. Suppose — and it is only hypothesis at this point — that *American monopoly capitalists were able to reduce a planned socialist Russia to the status of a captive technical colony? Would not this be the logical twentieth-century internationalist extension of the Morgan railroad monopolies and the Rockefeller petroleum trust of the late nineteenth century?*

"These are the rules of big business. They have superseded the teachings of our parents and are reducible to a simple maxim: Get a monopoly; let Society work for you: and remember that the best of all business is politics, **for a legislative grant, franchise, subsidy or tax exemption is worth more than a Kimberly or Comstock lode, since it does not require any labor, either mental or physical, for its exploitation"** (Frederick C. Howe, Confessions of a Monopolist, Chicago, Public Publishing, 1906), P. 157. From Chapter 1, **Wall Street and the Bolshevik Revolution by Antony Sutton** Arlington House, 1974.

The Published Works of Antony Sutton (See end of the APPENDEX) *WALL STREET AND THE BOLSHEVIK REVOLUTION WALL STREET AND THE RISE OF HITLER, by Antony C. Sutton* Gary Allen: *THE ROCKEFELLER FILE.doc* **Copy and past for internet search.**

ROBERT D. GORGOGLIONE SR.

THE ORIGINS OF
CORPORATE SOCIALISM

"Old John D. Rockefeller and his 19th century fellow-capitalists were convinced of one absolute truth: that **no great monetary wealth could be accumulated under the impartial rules of a competitive laissez faire society.** The only sure road to the acquisition of massive wealth was monopoly: Drive out your competitors, reduce competition, eliminate laissez-faire, and above all get state protection for your industry through compliant politicians and *government regulation. This last avenue yields a legal monopoly, and a legal monopoly always leads to wealth.*"

"This robber baron schema is also, under different labels, the socialist plan. The difference between a corporate state monopoly and a socialist state monopoly is essentially only the identity of the group controlling the power structure. *The essence of socialism is monopoly control by the state using hired planners and academic sponges.* On the other hand, Rockefeller, Morgan, and their corporate friends aimed to acquire and control their monopoly and to maximize its profits **through influence in the state political apparatus;** this, while it still needs hired planners and academic sponges, is a discreet and far more subtle process than outright state ownership under socialism. Success for the Rockefeller gambit has depended particularly upon focusing public attention upon largely irrelevant and superficial historical creations, such as the myth of a struggle between capitalists and communists, and careful cultivation of political forces by big business. We call this phenomenon of *corporate legal monopoly—market control acquired by using political influence—by the name of corporate socialism.*"

"The monopoly economic system based on **corruption and privilege** described by Howe is a **politically** run economy. It is at the same time also a system of disguised forced labor, called by Ludwig von Mises the *Zwangswirtschaft* system, a system of compulsion. *It is this element of compulsion that is common to all politically run economies:* Hitler's **New Order,** Mussolini's **corporate**

state, Kennedy's **New Frontier**, Johnson's **Great Society**, and Nixon's **Creative Federalism**. Compulsion was also an element in Herbert Hoover's reaction to the depression and much more obviously in Franklin D. Roosevelt's **New Deal** and the National Recovery Administration."

"It is this element of compulsion that **enables a few**—those who hold and gain from the **legal** monopoly—to live in society **at the expense of the many**. Those *who control or benefit from* the legislative franchises and regulation and who *influence the government bureaucracies* at the same time are **determining** the rules and regulations **to protect their present wealth, prey on the wealth of others,** *and keep out new entrants from their business.* "

"**In brief,** regulatory agencies are devices to use the police power of the state to *shield favored industries from competition, to protect their inefficiencies, and to guarantee their profits.* And, of course, these devices are vehemently defended by their wards: the regulated businessmen or, as we term them, '**the corporate socialists.**'" "This system of *legal compulsion* is the modern expression of **Frederic Bastiat's** dictum that *socialism is a system where everyone attempts to live at the expense of everyone else.* Consequently, corporate socialism is a system where those few who hold the *legal* monopolies of financial and industrial control, **profit** *at the expense of all others in society.* "

"**What was the philosophy of the financiers so far described?** Certainly anything but laissez-faire competition, which was the last system they envisaged. **Socialism, communism, fascism** or their variants were acceptable. The ideal for these financiers was "cooperation," forced if necessary. Individualism was out, and competition was immoral. On the other hand, cooperation was consistently advocated as moral and worthy, and nowhere is compulsion rejected as immoral. Why? **Because, when the verbiage is stripped away from the high-sounding phrases,** *compulsory cooperation was their golden road to a legal monopoly.* **Under the guise of public service, social objectives, and assorted do-goodism** *it is fundamentally 'Let society go to work for Wall Street.'*" (From Chapter 5 of *Wall Street and FDR* by **Antony Sutton**, Arlington House, 1975.) **See page 43,**

ROBERT D. GORGOGLIONE SR.

THE POLITICAL SPECTRUM

According to media and public education sources, our range of choices is defined within a spectrum of *far left, far right,* and the *rational middle ground*. The diagram looks something like this:

Fig. 5-3. The Popular Political Spectrum

Communism	The Sane Middle Ground	Fascism
International Socialism	Democratic Socialism	National Socialism

The far left is where those idealistic, but misguided communists hang out, and the far right is the dwelling place of those evil fascists. (Both of them use bullets as their primary means of directing public policy.) On the other hand, those in the "sane middle ground" seek many of the same ends as do the communists and fascists, but they are wise enough to use ballots instead of bullets. In theory, this prevents massive blood-letting every time political power changes hands. **As long as the losers believe that they can regain power later by using the system, ballots will not be replaced by bullets.**

What is interesting about this political spectrum is that **all the choices presented imply some form of socialism**. It is truly a masterpiece of debate strategy because it frames the debate in such a way that only one rational choice can be made. With all other choices excluded from consideration, the debate has been framed in advance **and the conclusions are fore-ordained.**

Another way of looking at our range of choices is in terms of the degree or percentage of government control of peoples' everyday lives:

Fig. 5-4. Government Power Spectrum

Total Government		All Variations in Between		No Government
Communism & Fascism	Socialism	Democratic Socialism	Constitutional Republic	Anarchy

In this figure, our range starts with ***total government*** on the left and ends with ***no government*** on the right. You will notice that Fascism (including Nazism) are ***left wing***, not right wing. **Both are *Socialistic*.**

Unlike *Figure 5-3*, *Figure 5-4* dramatically expands the conceptual framework by including more types of government. **This is important because it is hard to make wise choices when we do not fully understand what our options are.**

Should we even *have faith in constitutional government?*

MORE ON THE POLITICAL SPECTRUM

By G. Edward Griffin

We hear a lot today about right-wingers versus left-wingers, **but what do those terms really mean?** For example, we are told that communists and socialists are at the extreme left, and the Nazis and fascists are on the extreme right. Here we have the image of two powerful ideological adversaries pitted against each other, and the impression is that, somehow, they are opposites. But, what is the difference? **They are not opposites at all. They are the same.** The insignias may be different, but when you analyze communism and Nazism, **they both embody the principles of socialism.** Communists make no bones about socialism being their ideal, and the Nazi movement in Germany was actually called the National **Socialist** Party. Communist believe in *international* socialism, whereas Nazis advocate *national* socialism. Communists promote *class* hatred and *class* conflict to motivate the loyalty and blind obedience of their followers, whereas the Nazis use *race* conflict and *race* hatred to accomplish the same objective. Other than that, there is no difference between communism and Nazism. They are **both the epitome of collectivism**, and yet we are told they are, supposedly, at opposite ends of the spectrum!

There's only one thing that makes sense in constructing a political spectrum and that is to **put zero government at one end of the line and 100% at the other.** Now we have something we can comprehend. Those who believe in zero government are the **anarchists**, and those who believe in total government are the **totalitarians.** With that definition, we find that **communism and Nazism are together at the same end. They are both totalitarian.** Why? Because **they are both based on the model of collectivism.** Communism, Nazism, Fascism and socialism **all gravitate toward bigger and bigger government, because that is the logical extension of their common ideology.** Under collectivism, all problems are the responsibility of the state and must be solved by the state. The more problems there are, the more powerful you reach all the way to the end of the scale, which is total government. **Regardless of what name you give it, regardless of how you re-label it to make it seem new or different, *collectivism is totalitarianism.***

Actually, the straight-line concept of a political spectrum is somewhat misleading. It is really a circle. You can take that straight line with 100% government at one end and zero at the other, bend it around, and touch the ends at the top. Now it's a circle because, under anarchy, where there is no government, you have absolute rule by those with the biggest fists and the most powerful weapons. **So, you jump from zero government to totalitarianism in a flash.** They meet at the top. We are really dealing with a circle, and the only logical place for us to be is somewhere in the middle of the extremes. **We need social and political organization, of course, but it must be built on individualism**, an ideology with an affinity to that part of the spectrum **with the *least* amount of government possible instead of collectivism with an affinity to the other end of the spectrum with the *most* amount of government possible. That government is best which governs *least*.**

G. Edward Griffin at *www.freedomforceinternational.com*

Banks and Corporations: A Threat to Liberty

"I believe that banking institutions are more dangerous to our liberties than standing armies. If the American people ever allow private banks to control the issue of their currency, first by inflation, then by deflation, the banks and corporations that will grow up around [the banks] *will deprive the people of all property until their children wake-up homeless on the continent their fathers conquered.*" +

Thomas Jefferson

POLITICAL SYSTEMS

Why a Republic? The Flaws of Direct Democracy

**From an "Overview of Our World" by John F. McManus
President of the John Birch Society *www.jbs.org***

What is a Democracy?

Democracy is the rule of the majority or "mob rule". It means that if more than 50% of the group want something, they can have it but at the same time, the minority lose all their rights. Some call it "mobocracy" or **"tyranny of the majority"**.

Contrary to popular belief, the United States of America is not a democracy. Recall the Pledge of Allegiance, "I pledge allegiance to the flag of the United States of America and to the *republic* for which it stands . . . ."

The fundamental difference between a democracy and a republic is that if someone or a group of people came up to you and said that they were going to take away your home or business or children, you'd probably stand up and say, "No, you can't do that! I have my rights protected by the Constitution of the United States of America." And if you said that, you'd be describing a republic.

History has shown that democracies are fatally flawed and have consistently ended up as oligarchies. Therefore a Democratic system of government is only temporary. **It is in a transitional state which always ends in tyranny.** Therefore a Democracy is not a viable political system.

There are different styles of Government. However, there are really only two stable political systems—Oligarchy and Republic. The others are merely transitional states of governing.

Monarchy—Rule by One . . . but it does not *appear* as "Rule by One". **Canada is a perfect example!** In a convoluted way, in Canada the Monarchy controls at arms length through its representatives, the Governor General and the Prime Minister who swear their allegiances to the Crown but not to the flag, the people nor the nation that it stands for. The Prime Minister derives his power to overrule the MPs in Parliament from the Monarchy. The Prime Minister is never elected by the People. The reality is that it is "Rule by an elite group" with one up front. (Kings, potentates, Emperors, etc.).

Democracy—As soon as more people want something than don't, a tyranny of a democracy occurs (mobocracy). History has shown that all Democracies deteriorate into tyranny. Therefore, a Democracy is not a stable form of government but only a **transitional state toward an Oligarchy**, then revolution into anarchy and the cycle continues to repeat itself. (See page 38)

In 1787, Alexander Tyler, a Scottish history professor at the University of Edinborough, had this to say about "The Fall of Athenia" some 2,000 years prior:

> *A democracy is always temporary in nature; it simply cannot exist as a permanent form of government. A democracy will continue to exist up until the time that voters discover that they can vote themselves generous gifts from the public treasury. From that moment on, the majority (mobocracy) always votes for the candidates who promise the most benefits from the public treasury, with the result **that every democracy will finally collapse due to loose fiscal policy,** [which is] **always followed by a dictatorship.***

The United State's War Department's 1928 "Training Manual No. 2000-25," which was intended for use in citizenship training, defined democracy as:

> *A government of the masses. Authority derived through mass meeting or any other form of "direct expression." Results in mobocracy. **Attitude toward property is communistic** — negating property rights. Attitude of the law is that the will of the majority shall regulate, whether it be based upon deliberation or governed*

ROBERT D. GORGOGLIONE SR.

by passion, prejudice, and impulse, without restraint or regard to consequences.
Results in demagogism, license, agitation, discontent, anarchy.

James Madison, who is rightly known as the "Father of the Constitution," wrote in *The Federalist*, No. 10:

> "... *democracies have ever been spectacles of turbulence and contention; have ever been found incompatible with personal security, or the rights of property; and* ***have in general been as short in their lives as they are violent in their deaths.*** *" Democracy in America: TOC* by **Alexis de Tocqueville**

Republic—Rule by Law. The word Republic (res publica), which literally translated means law for the people (rule of objective law). A true republic is one that starts out by recognizing that individuals have rights, and so the limitation in the law is not upon the people but upon the government and the mob and the majority. (See pages 38 and 39)

Anarchy—The truth is that most crimes in history have been performed by Government, therefore occasionally people conclude that they want no government at all so they destroy the existing government with an uprising or a coup. This results in chaos, looting, burning, killing. This is not a true form of government as it is merely a transition where the people eventually ask for someone to come in and restore order and quite often it is the oligarchy which was overthrown in the first place, hence a return to an Oligarchy form of government. This happened in Russia in 1917, in Nicaragua in 1979 and in Iran in 1979. It has happened throughout history with great frequency. *Oligarchy* which is rule by a group, is the most common form of government in all history and it is the most common form of government today. A powerful few rule most of the nations of the world and therefore Oligarchy remains.

Types of Government

Monarchy	Oligarchy	Democracy	Republic	Anarchy
Rule by **One**	Rule by **Elite**	Rule by **Majority**	Rule by **Law**	Rule by **None**
Monarchies do not exist. Others are required to assist the person in charge; therefore, they share power.	**Examples:** Russia 1917 Hitler during WWII Nicaragua 1979 Iran 1979	**Example:** The Greek city states before Christ (B.C.). **A transitional form of government from one to another.**	**Example:** **U.S.A., according to its federal Constitution.**	**Only exists for a short period** of time, existing between democracy and republic or oligarchy. **Standing governments are either a republic or an oligarchy.**

Article IV Section 4 of the Constitution states: *"The United States shall guarantee to every State in this Union a Republican form of Government, and shall protect each of them against Invasion . . . "* ***A Republic, If You Can Keep It Republican Principles***

REPUBLICS VS DEMOCRACIES

By G. Edward Griffin

In recent years, we have been taught to believe that a democracy is the ideal form of government. Supposedly, that is what was created by the American Constitution. **But, if you read the documents and the speech transcripts of the men who *wrote* the Constitution, you find that they spoke very poorly of democracy.** They said in plain words that a democracy was one of the worst possible forms of government. And so they created what they called a republic. That is why **the word democracy doesn't appear anywhere in the Constitution;** and, when Americans pledge allegiance to the flag, it's to the *republic* for which it stands, not the democracy.

The difference between a democracy and a republic is the difference between collectivism and individualism. In a pure democracy, the majority rules; end of discussion. You might say, "What's wrong with that?" Well, there could be *plenty* wrong with that. What about a lynch mob? There is only one person with a dissenting vote, and he is the guy at the end of the rope. That's pure democracy in action.

"Ah, wait a minute," you say. "The majority should rule. Yes, but not to the extent of denying the rights of the minority," and, of course, you would be correct. That is precisely what a republic accomplishes. **A republic is a government based on the principle of *limited* majority rule so that the minority**—even a minority of one—will be protected from the whims and passions of the majority. Republics are often characterized by written constitutions that spell out the rules to make that possible. That was the functions of the American Bill of Rights, which is nothing more than a list of things the government may not do. It says that **Congress, even though it represents the majority, shall pass no law denying the minority their rights** to free exercise of religion, freedom of speech, peaceful assembly, the right to bear arms, and other "unalienable" rights.

These limitations on majority rule are the essence of a republic, and they also are at the core of the ideology called individualism. And so here is another major difference between these two concepts: Collectivism on the one hand, supporting any government actions so long as it can be said to be for the greater good of the greater number; and **individualism on the other hand, defending the rights of the minority against the passions and greed of the majority.** *www.freedomforceinternational.org*

THE ESSENCE OF A REPUBLIC

Checks & Balances

The powers the people granted to the three branches of government were specifically limited. Originally, the Constitution permitted few powers to the federal government, these chiefly being, as **Thomas Jefferson said,**

> the powers concerning *"war, peace, negotiation and distributing to every one exactly the functions he is competent to. Let the national government be entrusted with the defence of the nation, and its foreign and federal relations;* **the State governments with the civil rights, law, police, and administration of what concerns the State generally, the counties with the local concerns of the counties, and each ward direct the interests within itself.** *It is by dividing and subdividing these republics from the great national one down through all its subordinations . . . that all will be done for the best.* **What has destroyed liberty and the rights of man in every government which has ever existed under the sun? The generalizing and concentrating all cares and powers into one body."**

The Founding Fathers well understood human nature and its tendency to exercise unrighteous dominion when given authority. A Constitution was therefore designed to limit government to certain enumerated functions, beyond which was tyranny. (***The Constitution: A Heavenly Banner,*** **Deseret Books, Salt Lake City, Utah, 1986)**

THREE PRIMARY TYPES
OF CAPITALISM

They consist of *Competitive* and *Monopoly* Capitalism

1. ***Free-Market Capitalism (Competitive)***—Tools of production (*private* property) are owned and controlled by private citizens—***Constitutional Republic***

2. ***Government Controlled Capitalism (monopoly)***—Tools of production (*private* property) are owned by private citizens but controlled (regulated) by government—***Nazism and Fascism*** (Corporate Socialism).

3. ***Government-Owned Capitalism (monopoly)***—Tools of Production (property) are owned and thus controlled by government—***communism***

CAPITAL—MEANS OF PRODUCTION

(Tools, Machines, Working People)

Monopolistic Capitalism	Competitive Capitalism
Capital is controlled and/or owned **by the government.**	Capital is owned and controlled privately **by the citizens.**
Prices are **high**, like Poland in the '80s. Shortages (long lines exist for basic necessities). Certain individuals, or the government, control all capital for a type of business or service and therefore set prices and the level of production output.	**Prices** are **low**. Different businesses compete and therefore lower prices. There is an abundance of goods (ex., how many brands of detergent or cars are available in the U.S.A for purchase?).
Quality is **low**. With no competition, there is no initiative for improvement.	**Quality** is **high**. People buy the best products, which, logically, drives process improvement among competing producers.
No private property.	**Private property for all.**

Communism, socialism, Nazism, and fascism are all forms of **monopolistic** capitalism as apposed to **competitive *free enterprise*** capitalism.

Who chooses to live in a monopolistic society? Those who are too lazy to work against competition and too lazy to get competition underway.

Monopolistic state-controlled systems are the work of criminals who seize control of governments and set themselves up as monopoly producers for their own profit and power.

Four elements are required in order for you to have true private property:

- *Total ownership* (holding title)
- *Total control*
- *Total use*
- The ability to dispose of it as you see fit.

"The theory of the communists may be summed up in a single sentence: abolition of private property." Karl Marx, *The Communist Manifesto*, 1848

TYPES OF MONOPOLISTIC GOVERNMENTS

Communism Revolutionary Socialism	Socialism Example, England	Nazism National Socialism	Fascism Corporate Socialism
Government—controlled capital	Government-controlled capital	Government-controlled capital	Government-controlled capital
All capital owned by govt.	**Major** capital owned by govt.	**Some** capital owned by govt.	**No** capital owned by govt.
Example: Communism is socialism in a hurry. Example, The Union of Soviet Socialist Republics established socialism by means of a violent revolutionary seizure of power **and private property** and then creating and maintaining a police state. Government has begun to allow some "private" ownership of business, but they are controlled through **licensing and regulations.**	**Example:** Government-owned communications, transportation, utilities, export industry, banking industry, etc. Control of the rest of the economy is maintained through **licensing and regulations**. (Example, England). Those in favor of a socialist government want to get the citizens to vote themselves into socialism (no force).	**Example:** The Nazis owned Volkswagen but not other similar businesses; however, they controlled most of the businesses through government sanctioned cartels and through **licensing and regulations.**	**Example:** Mussolini said to the business owner, "I don't want to own your business. I just want to tell you what to produce, how much to produce, who to hire, who to fire, where to buy your raw materials, and what price to charge. The rest is up to you" People still think that they own their businesses but they are controlled through **licensing and regulations.** State sanctioned cartels controlled most businesses and industries.

From John F. McManus' *"Overview of Our World" www.jbs.org*

CLIPS FROM "THE LAW"

The Following excerpts from **Frederic Bastiat's** classic *THE LAW*, published in 1850, will give a greater insight into the *nature* and *principles* of socialism and its *consequences*.

Socialism Is Legal Plunder

"Now, legal plunder can be committed in an infinite number of ways. Thus we have an infinite number of plans for organizing it: tariffs, protection, *benefits, subsidies, encouragements, progressive taxation, public schools, guaranteed jobs, guaranteed profits, minimum wages, a right to relief, a right to the tools of labor, free credit,* and so on, and so on. All these plans as a whole —with their common aim of legal plunder — **constitute socialism.**

"Now, since under this definition socialism is a body of doctrine, what attack can be made against it other than a war of doctrine? If you find this socialistic doctrine to be false, absurd, and evil, then refute it. And the more false, the more absurd, and the more evil it is, the easier it will be to refute. *Above all, if you wish to be strong, begin by rooting out every particle of socialism that may have crept into your legislation.* This will be no light task.

"But it is upon the law that socialism itself relies. Socialists desire to practice legal plunder, not illegal plunder. *Socialists, like all other monopolists, desire to make the law their own weapon.* And when once the law is on the side of socialism, how can it be used against socialism? For when plunder is abetted by the law, it does not fear your courts, your gendarmes, and your prisons. *Rather, it may call upon them for help.*

"To prevent this, you would exclude socialism from entering into the making of laws? You would prevent socialists from entering the Legislative Palace?

You shall not succeed, I predict, *so long as legal plunder continues to be the main business of the legislature. It is illogical — in fact, absurd — to assume otherwise.*" (THE LAW, P. 22—23)

Try Liberty

"Away with their artificial systems! Away with the whims of governmental administrators, their socialized projects, their centralizations, their tariffs, their government schools, their state religions, their free credit, their bank monopolies, their regulations, their restrictions, their equalizations by taxation, and their pious moralizations!

"And now that the legislators and do-gooders have so futilely inflicted so many systems upon society, may they finally end where they should have begun: May they reject all systems, and try liberty; for liberty is an acknowledgement of faith in God and His works."

Proper Legislative Functions

"**It is not true that the legislator has absolute power over our persons and property**. The existence of persons and property preceded the existence of the legislator, and his function is only to guarantee their safety.

"**It is not true that the function of law is to regulate our consciences, our ideas, our wills, our education, our opinions, our work, our trade, our talents, or our pleasures**. The function of law is to protect the free exercise of these rights, and to prevent any person from interfering with the free exercise of these same rights by any other person.

"Since law necessarily requires the support of force, its lawful domain is only in the areas where the use of force is necessary. This is justice.

"**Every individual has the right to use force for lawful self-defense**. It is for this reason that the collective force — which is only the organized combination of the individual forces — may lawfully be used for the same purpose; and it cannot be used legitimately for any other purpose. "Law is solely the organization of the individual right of self—defense which existed before law was formalized. Law is justice."

The Law, by Frederic Bastiat Frederic Bastiat,
Ingenious Champion for Liberty and Peace | The . . .

And finally:

"*The State is the Great Fiction through which everybody endeavors to live at the expense of everybody* [else]."

"The State" by **Frederic Bastiat**

"*No man's life, liberty, or property are safe while the legislature is in session.*"

Learned Hand
New York Federal District Court Judge—1920s

ROBERT D. GORGOGLIONE SR.

CLIPS FROM "THE PROPER ROLE OF GOVERNMENT"

The following is taken from:

The Proper Role of Government
by the Honorable Ezra Taft Benson,
Secretary of Agriculture—1953-1961

Chapter 8 of *An Enemy Hath Done This,* 1969, Parliament Publishers
To study the *The Proper Role of Government*
go to *The **Proper Role of Government** & **The 5,000 Year Leap** (audio)
Freedom and Free Enterprise

Things the Government Should *Not* Do

"A category of government activity which, today, not only requires the closest scrutiny, but which also poses a grave danger to our continued freedom, is the activity NOT within the proper sphere of government. No one has the authority to grant such powers, as welfare programs, schemes for re-distributing the wealth, and activities which coerce people into acting in accordance with a prescribed code of social planning. **There is one simple test. Do I as an individual have a right to use force upon my neighbor to accomplish this goal? If I do have such a right, then I may delegate that power to my government to exercise on my behalf. If I do not have that right as an individual, then I cannot delegate it to government, and I cannot ask my government to perform the act for me.**

"To be sure, there are times when this principle of the proper role of government is most annoying and inconvenient. If I could only FORCE the ignorant to provide for themselves, or the selfish to be generous with their wealth! But if we permit government to manufacture its own authority out of thin air, and **to create self-proclaimed powers not delegated to it by the people, then the creature exceeds the creator and becomes master.** Beyond that point, where shall the line be drawn? Who is to say "this far, but no farther?" What clear PRINCIPLE will stay the hand of government from reaching farther and yet farther into our daily lives? We shouldn't forget the **wise words of President Grover Cleveland that** " . . . though the people support the Government **the Government should not support the people."** (P.P.N.S., p.345) **We should also remember, as Frederic Bastiat reminded us, that "Nothing can enter the public treasury for the benefit of one citizen or one class unless other citizens and other classes have been forced to send it in."** (THE LAW, P. 30; *Prophets, Principles and National Survival,* p.350, Publishers Press Salt Lake City, Utah, 191993)

The Dividing Line Between Proper and Improper Government

"As Bastiat pointed out over a hundred years ago, once government steps over this clear line between the protective or negative role into the aggressive role of redistributing the wealth and providing so-called "benefits" for some of its citizens, it then becomes a means for what he accurately described as *legalized plunder.* **It becomes a lever of unlimited power which is the sought-after prize of unscrupulous individuals and pressure groups, each seeking to control the machine to fatten his own pockets or to benefit its favorite charities**—*all with the other fellow's money, of course."* (THE LAW, 1850, reprinted by the Foundation for Economic Education, Irvington-On-Hudson, N.Y.)

The Nature of Legal Plunder

Listen to Bastiat's explanation of this *"legal plunder."*

> *"When a portion of wealth is transferred from the person who owns it—**without his consent** and without compensation, and whether by force or by fraud—**to anyone who does not own it,** then I say that property is violated; that an **act of plunder is committed!***

*"**How is the legal plunder to be identified?** Quite simply. See if the law takes from some persons what belongs to them, and gives it to other persons **to whom it does not belong.** See if the law benefits one citizen **at the expense of another** by doing what the citizen himself cannot do **without committing a crime . . .** "LAW, P. 21, 26; P.P.N.S., P. 377)*
Davy Crockett *vs. Welfare* **Davy Crockett's address to Congress**

As Bastiat observed, and as history has proven, **each class or special interest group competes with the others to throw the lever of governmental power in their favor**, or at least to immunize itself against the effects of a previous thrust. Labor gets a minimum wage, so agriculture seeks a price support. Consumers demand price controls, and industry gets protective tariffs. **In the end, no one is much further ahead, and everyone suffers the burdens of a gigantic bureaucracy and a loss of personal freedom.** With each group out to get its share of the spoils, such governments historically have mushroomed into total welfare states. Once the process begins, once the principle of the protective function of government gives way to the aggressive or redistribute function, **then forces are set in motion that drive the nation toward totalitarianism.**

"It is impossible," Bastiat correctly observed, "to introduce into society . . . a greater evil than this: **the conversion of the law into an instrument of plunder.**" (THE LAW, P. 12)

A Formula for Prosperity

The **principle behind the American philosophy of prosperity can be reduced to a rather simple formula:**

1. *Economic security for all is impossible without widespread abundance.*
2. *Abundance is impossible without industrious and efficient production*
3. *Such production is impossible without energetic, willing and eager labor*
4. *This is not possible without incentive.*
5. *Of all forms of incentive—the freedom to attain a reward for one's labors is the most sustaining for most people. Sometimes called THE PROFIT MOTIVE, it is simply the right to plan and to earn and to enjoy the fruits of your labor.*

6. *This profit motive DIMINISHES as government controls, regulations and taxes INCREASE to deny the fruits of success to those who produce.*
7. *Therefore, any attempt THROUGH GOVERNMENTAL INTERVENTION to redistribute the material rewards of labor can only result in the eventual destruction of the productive base of society, without which real abundance and security for more than the ruling elite is quite impossible.*

(*The Proper Role of Government* by Ezra Taft Benson, Chapter 30 of *God, Family and Country*, Deseret Books, 1974)

---

*"Still one thing more, fellow citizens—a wise and frugal government, which shall restrain men from injuring one another, which shall leave them **otherwise free to regulate their own pursuits of industry and improvement and shall not take from the mouth of labor the bread it has earned.** This is the sum of good government."*

Thomas Jefferson

CLIPS FROM "THE CONSTITUTION: A HEAVENLY BANNER"

The Following is taken from

The Constitution: A Heavenly Banner
by **the Honorable Ezra Taft Benson**
Secretary of Agriculture—1953-1961

Deseret Book Company, Salt Lake City, Utah
To study *The Constitution: A Heavenly Banner*

Go to *HEAVENLY BANNER.doc* and *PROTECTING
FREEDOM—BENS.*

The *Source* of Human Rights

The third important principle pertains to the source of basic human rights. **Thomas Paine,** back in the days of the American Revolution, explained:

> *"Rights are not gifts from one man to another, nor from one class of men to another . . . . It is impossible to discover any origin of rights otherwise than in the origin of man; it consequently follows that rights appertain to man in right of his existence, and must therefore be equal to every man."*

The great **Thomas Jefferson** asked:

> *"Can the liberties of a nation be thought secure when we have removed their only basis, a conviction in the minds of the people that **these liberties are of the gift of God**? that they are not to be violated but with his wrath?"*

The feelings of these great men are in keeping with the revelation of God through his prophet, who said:

> *"Men are free according to the flesh . . . and they are free to choose liberty and eternal life . . . or to choose captivity and death."* (2 Nephi 2:27.)

Rights are either *God-given* as part of the divine plan, or they are *granted by government* as part of the political plan. Reason, necessity, tradition, and religious conviction all lead me to accept the divine origin of these rights. **If we accept the premise that human rights are granted by government, then we must be willing to accept the corollary that they can be denied by government.** I, for one, shall never accept that premise. As the French political economist **Frederick Bastiat** phrased it so succinctly, *"Life, liberty, and property do not exist because men have made laws. On the contrary, it was the fact that life, liberty, property **existed beforehand** that caused men to make laws in the first place."*

We must ever keep in mind the inspired words of **Thomas Jefferson**, as found in the Declaration of Independence:

> *"We hold these truths to be self-evident, that all men are created equal, **that they are endowed by their Creator with certain unalienable Rights,** that among these are Life, Liberty and the pursuit of Happiness. That to secure these rights, Governments are instituted among Men, deriving their just powers from the consent of the governed."*

People Are *Superior* to Governments

The fourth basic principle we must understand is that people are superior to the governments they form. Since God created people with certain inalienable rights, and they, in turn, created government to help secure and safeguard those rights, it follows that the people are superior to the creature they created. **We are superior to government and should remain master over it,** not the other way around. Government is nothing more nor less than a relatively small group of citizens who have been hired, in a sense, by the rest of us to perform certain functions and discharge certain responsibilities we have authorized. **It stands to reason that the government itself has no**

innate power nor privilege to do anything. Its only source of authority and power is from the people who have created it. This is made clear in the **Preamble of the Constitution** of the United States, which reads:

> *WE THE PEOPLE*.... *do ordain and establish this Constitution for the United States of America"*

The Founders' Constitution: Table of Contents
Elliot's Debates The Federalist Papers The Records of the Federal Convention of 1787

RENEWAL OF ALLEGIANCE
TO THE CONSTITUTION

I wish to renew my declaration of allegiance to our divinely inspired Constitution, of which God Himself has said, *"I established the Constitution of this land by the hands of wise men whom I raised up unto this very purpose"* *(D&C 101:80), and about which Joseph, at the dedication of the Temple at Kirtland, prayed: "Have mercy, O Lord, upon all the nations of the earth; have mercy upon the rulers of our land; may those principles, which were so honorably and nobly defended, namely, the Constitution of our land, by our fathers, **be established forever.**"* **(D&C 109: 54)**

The Church more than a hundred years ago declared under Joseph's leadership:

> *"We believe that no government can exist in peace, **except** such laws are framed and held inviolate as will secure to each individual the free exercise of conscience, the right **and control** of property, and the protection of life."* **(D&C 134:2)**

Brigham Young [stated] . . . this *"Constitution of the people should be maintained for the rights and protection of all flesh, according to just and holy principles."*

No one can say that these rights and protections would be maintained if we lost representative government, and the will of one man or of a group were substituted therefore; nor if the mutual equality of citizens before the law were blotted out, and special privileges and rights and distinctions of class set up in place thereof; nor if property were destroyed or confiscated by the levying of taxes or under any other guise; nor if laws were passed which lay an unequal, oppressive hand upon the citizenry; nor if those sacred rights of freedom of speech, freedom of the press, freedom of religion, and of public assembly were curtailed or wiped out; nor if any of the other of our great guarantees and free institutions were torn out of our Constitution and snatched from our lives.

As I have said to you before, so I say again, **the Constitution** of the United States **is a great and treasured part of my religion,** and the revelations of the Lord and the words of our inspired leaders compel it to be so. The overturning, or the material changing, or the distortion of any fundamental principle of our Constitutional government **would thus do violence to my religion.**

President J. Reuben Clark Jr.
Stand Fast by Our Constitution, pp. 6-7, Deseret Book Co., SLC, 1962

"THE NEW WORLD ORDER"— A THREAT TO THE CONSTITUTION

*"**There is one and only one legitimate goal of United States foreign policy.** It is a narrow goal, a nationalistic goal: **the preservation of our national independence.** Nothing in the Constitution grants that the president shall have the privilege of offering himself as a world leader. He's our executive; he's on our payroll, if necessary; he's supposed to put our best interests in front of those of other nations. Nothing in the Constitution nor in logic grants to the President of the United States or to Congress the power to influence the political life of other countries, to "uplift" their cultures, to bolster their economies, to feed their peoples or even to defend them against their enemies."*

"Many well-intentioned people are now convinced that we are living in a period of history which makes it both possible and necessary to abandon our national sovereignty, to merge our nation militarily, economically, and politically with other nations, and to form, at last a world government which, supposedly, would put an end to war."

*"Sovereignty for a nation is hard to come by and even more difficult to retain. It cannot be shared, for then sovereignty becomes something else, and, for want of a better word, when sovereignty is lessened the end-product is internationalism. **Sovereignty is neither more nor less than self-government. American self-government is blueprinted in the Constitution.**"*

Ezra Taft Benson
Secretary of Agriculture, 1953-1961
"United States Foreign Policy"

*United States **Foreign Policy***, chap. 9 of ***An Enemy Hath Done This*** by Ezra Taft Benson, Parliament Publishers, Salt Lake City, Utah, 1969.
Also ***NEW WORLD ORDER—BENSON***.

GENERAL MORONI AND
THE TITLE OF LIBERTY

War in Heaven continues on Earth

Of course, the war in heaven over free agency is now being waged here on earth, and there are those today who are saying *"Look, don't get involved in the fight for freedom. Just live the gospel."* **That counsel is dangerous, self-contradictory, unsound.**

The Book of Mormon pays tribute to General Moroni in these words:

> *"And Moroni was a strong and a mighty man; he was a man of perfect understanding, yea, a man that did not delight in bloodshed; a **man whose soul did joy in the liberty and the freedom of his country, and his brethren from bondage and slavery;** . . .*

> *"Yea, and he was a man who **was firm in the faith of Christ**, and he **had sworn with an oath** to defend his people his rights, and his country, and his religion, **even to the loss of his blood."** (Al. 48:11,13.)*

> **And then Moroni is paid this high tribute:** *"Yea, verily, verily I say unto you, **if all men had been, and were, and ever would be, like unto Moroni behold, the very powers of hell would have been shaken forever; yea**, the devil would never have power over the hearts of the children of men."* (Al. 48:17.)

Now, part of the reason we may not have sufficient priesthood bearers to save the Constitution let alone to shake the powers of hell, is because unlike Moroni, **I fear, our souls do not joy in keeping our country free, and we are not firm in the faith of Christ nor have we sworn with an oath to defend our rights and the liberty of our country.** *PROTECTING FREEDOM—BENS.*

President Ezra Taft Benson
Protecting Freedom, October 2, 1966 General Conference

"Founded in the Wisdom of God"

Hence we say that the Constitution of the United States is a glorious standard; **it is founded in the wisdom of God. It is a heavenly banner;** *it is to all those who are privileged with the sweets of its liberty, like the cooling shades and refreshing waters of a great rock in a thirsty and weary land. It is like a great tree under whose branches men from every clime can be* **shielded from the burning rays of the sun**.

Joseph Smith
Liberty Jail, March 1839

Our Destiny

"Now may we follow the great example of our Founding Fathers and walk in their footsteps; pick up where they left off and **restore our divinely inspired Constitution**, *and thus our beloved country to its former greatness and glory; that* **we may once again be a shining light of Liberty and hope for a world in spiritual darkness and bondage—for this is our destiny!"**

Robert D. Gorgoglione
April 30, 2008

"[The United States Constitution was] *the entering wedge for the introduction of a new era and in it were introduced principles for the birth and organization of a new world."*

John Taylor
Journal of Discourses, Vol. 21, Page 31, April 9,

Wallstreet and FDR

By

Antony C. Sutton

Socialists on Wall Street

- Why many Wall Streeters who invested in the Bolshevik Revolution also bankrolled FDR

- The powerful men who commuted between the White House and 120 Broadway

- How Wall Street insiders turned the Federal Reserve System into a money machine for the elite

- FDR translates government contracts into personal profits: the case of the naval guns

- The international financiers who liked Mussolini and loved FDR

- Why some money men backed FDR in 1932

- The "Butler Affair": the truth about the plot to install a dictator in the White House

- How politics helped make FDR rich in the bond business

- Huey Long's prophetic warning about Bernard Baruch and other New Deal financiers

- How FDR tried to profit by hyperinflation in the Weimar Republic

- The NRA: Wall Street's reward for dumping Herbert Hoover?

- FDR's 11 corporate directorships

- Unearthed: the 1841 NRA-like scheme written by a 19th-century cousin of FDR

- How Wall Streeters in New Deal guise helped buy off Big Labor—then used it

- The Swope Plan: blueprint for the corporate state

- FDR's vending machine interests

- The three musketeers of the NRA. Their Wall Street ties

- FDR attempts to revolutionize the construction industry. Why he failed

- FDR's scheme to profit from confiscated German patents

- How the captains of industry running the NRA punished their fellow businessmen

- FDR's $200,000 debt to the money men

- Wall Street's attempt to create a private army of 500,000 men to "support the President"

- The dime's worth of difference between corporate socialists and radical socialists

- Strange facts surrounding the Warm Springs Foundation, FDR's biggest investment

- Was FDR really the friend of the common man?

Continued

WALL STREET AND THE RISE OF HITLER

By
Antony C. Sutton

TABLE OF CONTENTS

Chapter Four

Standard Oil Duels World War II

Ethyl Lead for the Wehrmacht
Standard Oil and Synthetic Rubber
The Deutsche-Amerikanische Petroleum A.G.

Chapter Five

I.T.T. Works Both Sides of the War

Baron Kurt von Schröder and I.T.T.
Westrick, Texaco, and I.T.T.
I.T.T. in Wartime Germany

PART TWO: Wall Street and Funds for Hitler

Chapter Six

Henry Ford and the Nazis

Henry Ford: Hitler's First Foreign Banker
Henry Ford Receives a Nazi Medal
Ford Assists the German War Effort

Chapter Seven

Who Financed Adolf Hitler?

Some Early Hitler Backers
Fritz Thyssen and W.A. Harriman Company
Financing Hitler in the March 1933 Elections
The 1933 Political Contributions

Chapter Eight

Putzi: Friend of Hitler and Roosevelt

Putzi's Role in the Reichstag Fire
Roosevelt's New Deal and Hitler's New Order

Continued

Wall Street and the Bolshevik Revolution

By

Antony C. Sutton

View enlarged picture

SUTTON'S RESEARCH REVEALS:

- The role of J. P. (Pontifex Maximus) Morgan banking executives in funneling illegal Bolshevik gold into the U.S.

- How the American Red Cross was coopted by powerful forces on Wall Street.

- Wall Streeters who intervened to free Leon Trotsky, even though Trotsky's stated aim was to engineer "the real revolution"— the Soviet coup which toppled Kerensky.

- The deals made by major corporations to capture the huge Russian market a decade and a half before the U.S. recognized the Soviet regime.

- The "closet socialism" of leading businessmen who paraded publicly as champions of free enterprise.

Continued

Table of Contents

Preface

THE BEST ENEMY
MONEY CAN BUY

By
Antony C. Sutton

TABLE OF CONTENTS

Chapter IV:

Soviets Buy into the 21st Century

Early Soviet Electronic Acquisitions
Bridging the Semi-conductor Gap
How the Deaf Mute Blindmen helped the
Soviets into the 21st Century
The Bruchhausen Network
The Type of Equipment Shipped to the USSR

Chapter V:

Computers—Deception by Control Data Corporation

Soviet Agatha—American Apple II
Military End Use
Control Data Deception
The Deceptive World View of Control Data Corporation

Chapter VI:

Soviet in the Air

German Assistance for Soviet Rockets
Sputnik, Lunik and the Soyuz Programs
Why Did the Soviets Embark on a Space Program?
Soviet Aircraft Development
Foreign Designs for Soviet Aircraft Engines
The Wright Cyclone Engine in the Soviet Union
Western Contribution to the Postwar Soviet Air Force
The Boeing B-20 Four-Engined Bomber becomes
the Tu-4 and the Tu-70
The First Soviet Jets
Development of the First Soviet Jet Engine
MIG Fighters Rolls-Royce Turbojets
The Supersonic Tu-144 (Alias "Konkordskiy")

Chapter VII:

The Deaf Mutes and the Soviet Missile Threat

American Acceleromters for Soviet Missiles
American Ball Bearings for Missile Guidance Systems

Chapter VIII:

The Soviets at Sea

Origins of the Soviet Merchant Marine
Illegal Actions by State Department
The Deaf Mute Blindmen Forge Ahead
Submarine and Anti-Submarine Warfare
The Soviet Union as a Source of Information

Chapter IX:

The Leaky Pipeline Embargo

Working Both Sides of the Street
The Reagan Administration Marshmallow Approach

Chapter X:

DMBs Supply Nerve Gas Plants

State Department Concurs in Explosives Manufacture
The DMB and Nerve Gas Technology

Chapter XI:

Chevron-Gulf Keeps Marxist Angola Afloat

Identification of the Deaf Mute Blindmen
What is to be done

Chapter XII:

Tanks

The Development of Soviet Tank Design
The Famous T-34 Medium Tank
DMB Pleas of Ignorance
The U.S.-Built Stalingrad "Tractor" Plant
The U.S.-Built Kharkov "Tractor" Plant
The U.S.-Built Chelyabinsk "Tractor" Plant

Chapter XIII:

Why the DMBs Aid Soviet Ambitions

The Bureaucrats' View of "Peaceful Trade"
Useless Pinpricks as Policy
Multinational Businessmen and the Politics of Greed

CONCLUSIONS:

Treason

Are the Soviets Enemies?
The Soviet Record of Aggression
Are the Deaf Mute Blindmen Guilty of Treason?
United States Constitution

APPENDIX A:

Exchange of Letters with Department of Defense, 1971

APPENDIX B:

Testimony of the Author Before Subcommittee VII of the Platform at Miami Beach, Florida, August 15,
1972, at 2:30 P.M.

APPENDIX C:

Letter from William C. Norris, Chairman of Control Data Corporation to Congressman Richard T. Hanna, 1973

APPENDIX D:

Letter from Fred Schlafly to friends and supporters of American Council for World Freedom, dated April 1978, asking to mail "Yellow Cards" of protest to William Norris
Letter from William C. Norris to each "Yellow Card Sender," dated May 5, 1978
Letter (Protocol) of Intent dated 19 October 1973 (English version) between State Committee of the USSR Council of Ministers for Science and Technology and the Control Data Corporation
English version of Agreement between State Committee of the Council of Ministers of the USSR for Science and Technology and Control Data Corporation (signe4d by Robert D. Schmidt), dated 19 October 1973

APPENDIX E:

Position of Texas Instruments Company and Chairman Fred Bucy on dangers of trading technology to the Soviets

APPENDIX F:

U.S. Firms Trading with the Soviet Union in the 1960-1985 Period

APPENDIX G:

Confidential Government Report on Cummins Engine Company (J. Irwin Miller) and Financing of Marxist Revolutionary Activities Within the United States.

APPENDIX H:
From the Phoenix Letter, January 1986 Issue

APPENDIX I:

U.S. Weapons Technology Sold To Soviets

The End

www.ingramcontent.com/pod-product-compliance
Lightning Source LLC
Chambersburg PA
CBHW020334290526
45785CB00005B/2010